Mission Trip Journal

This 14 Day Journal Belongs To:

_____

_____

Mission Trip Journal
by Paul L. Slater
© 2019

The World English Bible (WEB) is a Public Domain Modern English translation of the Holy Bible.

Mission Trip Journal for Up to 14 Days

Journaling Day 2   Date _____

How did God speak to you through Scripture today?

_____
_____
_____
_____
_____
_____

Where did God lead you today geographically?

_____
_____
_____
_____
_____

What has challenged your faith the most today and how can God use it in your life and ministry?

_____
_____
_____
_____
_____

Who was it that God led you to minister to today and what was their response?

_____
_____
_____
_____

Document the details of your mission trip so that you can recall all that happened.

...ed to you today and how did God use

_____
_____
_____
_____
_____
_____

...tual lesson you learned today?

_____
_____
_____
_____
_____
_____

Share the biggest "take-away" from this day that will remind you of God's grace and faithfulness:

_____
_____
_____
_____
_____
_____
_____
_____
_____
_____
_____

Make daily entries to enable you to remember what God did so that you can share those experiences with others.

More Sample Pages 14 Day Mission Trip Journal

My Mission Trip Team

"He is no fool who gives up what he cannot keep to gain that which he cannot lose" — Jim Elliot

Contact Information and Impressions of Your Time Together
Doodle or Draw a Picture of What you Want to Remember

Pages for your Team Members to write their contact information. They can also share their impressions of your mission adventure. Use this space to doodle or draw too.

Daily Schedule
Date___/___/_____

12 pm	
1 pm	
2 pm	
3 pm	
4 pm	
5 pm	
6 pm	
7 pm	
8 pm	
9 pm	

There is a Daily Schedule page for keeping track of meetings, activities and appointments. Allow time for your journaling too.

Pages to Report Back All that God Did

There are blank pages for reporting back what God did on this mission trip.

It is so easy to forget travel details or times of spiritual significance if you don't write them down.

People will ask you to share "What Happened?" Because you took time to document each day's activities, you will be able to report all that God did through you and your team.

You can draw upon what you wrote in this journal. This is your resource for what you will share when you report back.

You will be able to tell about changed lives because of God's love and grace impacting people.

You wrote the names of team members and also those you ministered to.

You recorded travel information, events and work details, so include them in your report.

Events, People, and Places I Want to "Report Back"

_____
_____
_____
_____
_____
_____
_____
_____
_____
_____
_____
_____
_____
_____
_____
_____
_____
_____
_____
_____
_____
_____
_____
_____
_____
_____
_____

Finally, share how you have been changed because you have seen God work miracles. Testify what the Lord is doing spiritually within you because of this trip.

How to Use This Mission Trip Journal

Journal to Document the Fingerprints of God
The Book of Acts in the New Testament is a mission trip journal. As we read chapters 13 through 28, we see Luke describing the missionary journeys of Apostle Paul and his mission team.

Perhaps Luke's first intention was that his journal entries were written for himself to read later, reminding him how God was working in his life and in the lives of those with whom he traveled.

Journal to Document Pre-Mission Trip Miracles
A part of every mission trip is realizing what God did before the trip began, events and situations that indicated He wanted you to go on this trip. Answer these questions:

- What were some of the challenges you faced in order to go?
- How did God call you to this particular assignment and what did He do in preparing you to hear that call?
- What were some of the obstacles God had to overcome within you for you hear His voice to go?
- How did God provide the financial resources for you to go?

Journal to Document Travel Experiences Worth Sharing
As we explore the 13th chapter of Acts, we learn that this was the first of many trips of Paul that were documented by Luke. Notice he includes several key components that are true of all mission trips.

In the pages of this journal you will find opportunity to record the same components that Luke included in his mission trip journals, namely, What God Is doing to and through you.

- **How did God speak to you through scripture today**? It is easy to be so busy for the Lord that we forget to listen for His instructions for the day.
- **Where did God lead you geographically today?** Luke found it important to specify where it was that God led them and so should you.

- The next question to journal is a reminder that God is working in you as well as through you: **Who did God choose to minister to you and how did they do so?**
- And yes, your mission trip is not just about geographical locations but about the people you find there. So answer this question: **To whom did God lead you to minister to today and in what way?**
- **What has challenged your faith the most today?** This question gives you opportunity to express your honest feelings that arise whenever people work together or do not respond in the way you expected.
- **What is the greatest spiritual lesson you learned today?** God has you on this trip to stretch you and grow you into Christlikeness.
- Conclude your daily journal by **sharing the biggest "take-away" for the day**. You are describing what God is doing in your life that will become part of your testimony to others as well as a reminder to yourself of God's grace and faithfulness.

Share With Others What God Did for You

Use these entries to share what God has done through any speaking or writing opportunities that the Lord opens up for you. One of the key concepts following the mission trips of Paul in the Book of Acts was "reporting back what God had done."

Acts 14:24-27 WEB
*They passed through Pisidia, and came to Pamphylia. (25) When they had spoken the word in Perga, they went down to Attalia. (26) From there they sailed to Antioch, from where they had been committed to the grace of God for the work which they had fulfilled. (27) When they had arrived, and had gathered the assembly together, **they reported all the things that God had done with them, and that he had opened a door of faith to the nations.***

May God open up opportunities for you to report back to your church what God has done through this mission trip experience. And because of this journal, you will now know what to say.

My Mission Trip Expectations

What do I anticipate most about this mission trip?

_____

_____

_____

_____

_____

What do I want God to do spiritually in my life?

_____

_____

_____

_____

Who do I have praying for me and my mission trip team?

_____

_____

_____

_____

How do I see God using this trip in my church?

_____

_____

_____

_____

Mission Trip Travel Checklist

Before Packing:

- Liquids, gels and aerosols packed in carry-on must follow the 3-1-1 liquids rule: 3.4 ounces or less per container
- 1-quart size, clear, plastic, zip top bag (all liquids must fit in bag)
- Find out how many bags per passenger your carrier allows.
- Review the prohibited items list for both carry-on and checked baggage.
- If purchasing a baggage lock, be sure to look for those that are TSA recognized.
- Tape a card with your name and contact information on your electronics.

When Packing:

- Pack items in layers (shoes one layer, clothes one layer, electronics one layer, etc.)
- Firearms are only allowed in checked baggage and must be unloaded, placed in a locked, hard-sided container and declared to your airline.
- All fireworks contain explosive materials and are not permitted in checked or carry-on baggage.
- Pack large electronics on top layer of carry-on for screening accessibility.
- Place your 3-1-1 bag with liquids, gels and aerosols in the front pocket of your carry-on for accessibility.
- If traveling with a pet, be sure to bring a leash so carriers can be properly screened.
- Before Leaving for the Airport
- Give yourself enough time to arrive at the airport early.
- Wear easily removable shoes.
- Passengers with a disability or medical condition may call ahead to the TSA Cares toll free helpline at (855) 787-2227.

Before Entering the Checkpoint

- ϒ Eligible passengers look for the TSA Pre-check lane for expedited screening at participating airports.
- ϒ Have your ID and boarding pass out for inspection.
- ϒ In the screening lane remove the 3-1-1 liquids bag and place it in the bin.
- ϒ Ensure pockets are empty (keys, tissues, currency, wallets, cell phones, etc.) and remove bulky jewelry (valuable items can be placed in carry-on).
- ϒ If required, remove your shoes and place them directly on the X-ray belt.
- ϒ Remove personal electronic devices larger than a cell phone from your carry-on bag and place them into a bin with nothing placed on or under them for X-ray screening. (E.g. laptops, tablets, e-readers and handheld game consoles.)
- ϒ Remember to check the bins and collect all belongings after going through screening.

For the latest requirements go to the State Department website by searching for "travel checklist gov" or go to **https://travel.state.gov/content/travel/en/international-travel/before-you-go/travelers-checklist.html**

Know the Baggage Rules On International Travel

How Many Bags Are Allowed On an International Flight?

That is a great question to ask for the mission trip traveler. But remember that for most of us, we fly domestic flights first to get to the international leg of the trip so know those rules too.

The answer depends on the airline; for many airlines, the answer further depends on the class of service, the route flown, and the passenger's frequent flier status.

Call Your Particular Airline or Check Their Website

If you are travelling with more than one airline you should also make sure your bag allowance is in the guidelines of each airline.

There are specific rules for most major American carriers, however you should check with the airline you intend to fly because each one differs.

Understand There are Rules Regarding Baggage

Generally at the time of this writing, you are allowed 2 checked bags (both going into the cargo hold), 1 carry-on, and one personal item (these 2 items to go on the plane with you). For most carriers, checked bags cannot exceed 62 linear inches (height + length + depth).

Realize that each country has their own set of rules. Even though most countries allow you to bring the amounts specified above, there are countries that limit the traveler to only 1 checked bag. Also, during certain times of year there can be limitations due to excess traffic.

What Can Be Done to Make Luggage Costs More Affordable?

First of all, travel light! You will be working. Do understand that there could be dress codes you should know as to what is appropriate to wear in specific cultures.

Frequent flier programs and Airline reward programs may allow you to bring extra luggage. For example, with many frequent flier programs you can bring two checked bags for free.

If there are veterans and dependents of active duty, Reserve military or National Guard on your mission trip team, they often get up to three pieces of checked baggage under 40 pounds for free and no charge for oversized checked baggage. Sometimes the whole team may get those benefits if they are travelling together. Just ask to see if this is a possibility.

Regarding the use of credit cards that provide travel benefits such as free checked baggage. Common sense suggests that you promise to PAY OFF THE BALANCE EACH MONTH. With high interest charges on many of these cards, it is never worth the miles or points if the monthly finance charge wipes out the financial benefit.

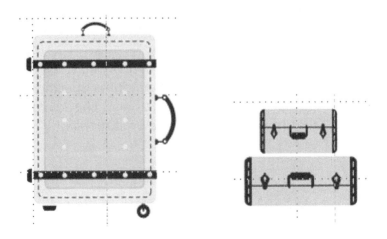

Faith-Based Travelers

Before You Go
Visit **https://travel.state.gov/** to review specific country information pages for details on visa requirements and to learn about some local laws that may impact you.

U.S. faith-based travelers, in addition to being aware of basic country conditions that impact all travelers, should know that in some countries there are laws about religious activities. You need to know the laws and conditions in the places you will be living and traveling.

Sponsoring Organization Travel Requirements
- Does it have plans for various emergency scenarios, such as local threats to security, natural disasters, and injury or death of a U.S. citizen traveler?
- Is it aware of laws and customs about religious expression in the countries you will be visiting?
- Is your sponsoring organization a member of the Overseas Security Advisory Council, either in the United States or in your destination country?
- If your organization's travel itinerary include trips to an orphanage please read the warnings about "voluntourism" at orphanages.

Know the Laws About Religious Expression
Many countries have laws that restrict religious expression, such as:
- public or private prayer or other religious practices
- wearing religious attire or symbols
- preaching in a private or public setting
- speaking to others about your beliefs
- possessing religious images
- criticizing or questioning the religious beliefs of others
- visiting certain religious sites if you are female
- possessing printed religious materials
- distributing religious literature; and
- participating in religious services or activities.

There is information on how to contact the U.S. embassy or consulate at **https://travel.state.gov/** .

Pre-Mission Trip Miracles

What led you to go on this particular mission trip?

_____

_____

_____

_____

_____

What were some of the challenges you faced in order to go?

_____

_____

_____

_____

_____

How did God provide resources for you to go?

_____

_____

_____

_____

_____

How has God prepared you for this specific mission trip?

_____

_____

_____

_____

_____

Faith-Based Travelers STEP Enrollment

What is STEP?
The Smart Traveler Enrollment Program (STEP) is a free service to allow U.S. citizens and nationals traveling and living abroad to enroll their trip with the nearest U.S. Embassy or Consulate.

Benefits of Enrolling in STEP:
- Receive important information from the Embassy about safety conditions in your destination country, helping you make informed decisions about your travel plans.
- Help the U.S. Embassy contact you in an emergency, whether natural disaster, civil unrest, or family emergency.

Register at https://step.state.gov/step/

Reasons to Register:
- Help family and friends get in touch with you in an emergency.

- If you run into problems while overseas, contact the nearest U.S. embassy or consulate. Consular officers in the American Citizens Services office may be able to help if you run into problems overseas, especially if you feel you cannot approach local police, or if you need help communicating with local authorities.

Continue to the next page for Safety Preparation Information and spaces to write the specific Embassy information for the countries you will be visiting.

24 Hour Consular Emergency Line: U.S. 1.888.407.4747 / Outside the U.S. 1.202.501.4444

U.S. faith-based travelers, in addition to being aware of basic country conditions that impact all travelers, should know the laws and conditions in the places you will be living and traveling.

For example, did you know that in some countries it is a crime to conduct religious activities! You need to be aware of what is allowed as to the laws and the cultural norms of your destinations.

Safety Preparation for Your Mission Trip

You need to be prepared for emergencies that could take place. There could be political unrest or legal difficulties that arise. Medical emergencies are always a possibility as are weather-related tragedies.

What if the emergencies are back home and someone needs to contact you. You can be prepared for these situations by accessing the State Department website. There is an extensive list located at **https://www.usembassy.gov** for you to find specific country information.

Instructions:
1. Find the Address and Phone Number of the U.S. Embassy or Consulate for the various countries you will be visiting.
2. Write the information for the countries you will be visiting into your Mission Trip Journal. The following page contains more entry blanks for you to use.

Country	
Address	
City	
Telephone	

Country	
Address	
City	
Telephone	

U.S. Embassy Information (continued)

Country	
Address	
City	
Telephone	

Country	
Address	
City	
Telephone	

Country	
Address	
City	
Telephone	

Always carry the address and phone number of the U.S. embassy or consulate with you, in English and the local language.

Once again, you need to know that Consular officers in the American Citizens Services office may be able to help if you run into problems overseas, especially if you feel you cannot approach local police, or if you need help communicating with local authorities.

This is because consular officers will not make generalizations, assumptions, or pass judgment, and will work to safeguard your privacy under applicable U.S. laws and policies.

Daily Schedule
Day 1 Date___/___/_____

6 am	
7 am	
8 am	
9 am	
10 am	
11 am	
12 pm	
1 pm	
2 pm	
3 pm	
4 pm	
5 pm	
6 pm	
7 pm	
8 pm	
9 pm	

Journaling Day 1   Date _____

How did God speak to you through Scripture today?

_____

_____

_____

_____

_____

_____

Where did God lead you today geographically?

_____

_____

_____

_____

_____

What has challenged your faith the most today and how can God
use it in your life and ministry?

_____

_____

_____

_____

_____

Who was it that God led you to minister to today and what was
their response?

_____

_____

_____

_____

_____

_____

Who was it that ministered to you today and how did God use them in your life?

_____

_____

_____

_____

_____

_____

_____

What is the greatest spiritual lesson you learned today?

_____

_____

_____

_____

_____

_____

Share the biggest "take-away" from this day that will remind you of God's grace and faithfulness:

_____

_____

_____

_____

_____

_____

_____

_____

_____

_____

_____

Daily Schedule
Day 2 Date____/____/_____

6 am	
7 am	
8 am	
9 am	
10 am	
11 am	
12 pm	
1 pm	
2 pm	
3 pm	
4 pm	
5 pm	
6 pm	
7 pm	
8 pm	
9 pm	

Journaling Day 2   Date _____

How did God speak to you through Scripture today?

_____

_____

_____

_____

_____

_____

Where did God lead you today geographically?

_____

_____

_____

_____

_____

What has challenged your faith the most today and how can God use it in your life and ministry?

_____

_____

_____

_____

_____

_____

Who was it that God led you to minister to today and what was their response?

_____

_____

_____

_____

_____

Who was it that ministered to you today and how did God use them in your life?

_____
_____
_____
_____
_____
_____
_____

What is the greatest spiritual lesson you learned today?

_____
_____
_____
_____
_____
_____

Share the biggest "take-away" from this day that will remind you of God's grace and faithfulness:

_____
_____
_____
_____
_____
_____
_____
_____
_____
_____
_____

Daily Schedule
Day 3 Date____/____/_____

6 am	
7 am	
8 am	
9 am	
10 am	
11 am	
12 pm	
1 pm	
2 pm	
3 pm	
4 pm	
5 pm	
6 pm	
7 pm	
8 pm	
9 pm	

Journaling Day 3   Date _____

How did God speak to you through Scripture today?

_____
_____
_____
_____
_____
_____

Where did God lead you today geographically?

_____
_____
_____
_____
_____

What has challenged your faith the most today and how can God use it in your life and ministry?

_____
_____
_____
_____
_____
_____

Who was it that God led you to minister to today and what was their response?

_____
_____
_____
_____
_____
_____

Who was it that ministered to you today and how did God use them in your life?

_____

_____

_____

_____

_____

_____

_____

What is the greatest spiritual lesson you learned today?

_____

_____

_____

_____

_____

_____

Share the biggest "take-away" from this day that will remind you of God's grace and faithfulness:

_____

_____

_____

_____

_____

_____

_____

_____

_____

_____

_____

_____

Daily Schedule

Day 4 Date___/___/_____

6 am	
7 am	
8 am	
9 am	
10 am	
11 am	
12 pm	
1 pm	
2 pm	
3 pm	
4 pm	
5 pm	
6 pm	
7 pm	
8 pm	
9 pm	

Journaling Day 4   Date _____

How did God speak to you through Scripture today?

_____
_____
_____
_____
_____
_____

Where did God lead you today geographically?

_____
_____
_____
_____
_____

What has challenged your faith the most today and how can God use it in your life and ministry?

_____
_____
_____
_____
_____
_____

Who was it that God led you to minister to today and what was their response?

_____
_____
_____
_____
_____
_____

Who was it that ministered to you today and how did God use them in your life?

_____

_____

_____

_____

_____

_____

_____

What is the greatest spiritual lesson you learned today?

_____

_____

_____

_____

_____

_____

Share the biggest "take-away" from this day that will remind you of God's grace and faithfulness:

_____

_____

_____

_____

_____

_____

_____

_____

_____

_____

_____

Daily Schedule
Day 5 Date___/___/_____

6 am	
7 am	
8 am	
9 am	
10 am	
11 am	
12 pm	
1 pm	
2 pm	
3 pm	
4 pm	
5 pm	
6 pm	
7 pm	
8 pm	
9 pm	

Journaling Day 5   Date _____

How did God speak to you through Scripture today?

_____
_____
_____
_____
_____
_____

Where did God lead you today geographically?

_____
_____
_____
_____
_____

What has challenged your faith the most today and how can God use it in your life and ministry?

_____
_____
_____
_____
_____
_____

Who was it that God led you to minister to today and what was their response?

_____
_____
_____
_____
_____
_____

Who was it that ministered to you today and how did God use them in your life?

_____

_____

_____

_____

_____

_____

_____

What is the greatest spiritual lesson you learned today?

_____

_____

_____

_____

_____

_____

Share the biggest "take-away" from this day that will remind you of God's grace and faithfulness:

_____

_____

_____

_____

_____

_____

_____

_____

_____

_____

_____

Daily Schedule
Day 6 Date___/___/_____

6 am	
7 am	
8 am	
9 am	
10 am	
11 am	
12 pm	
1 pm	
2 pm	
3 pm	
4 pm	
5 pm	
6 pm	
7 pm	
8 pm	
9 pm	

Journaling Day 6   Date _____

How did God speak to you through Scripture today?

_____

_____

_____

_____

_____

_____

Where did God lead you today geographically?

_____

_____

_____

_____

_____

What has challenged your faith the most today and how can God use it in your life and ministry?

_____

_____

_____

_____

_____

_____

Who was it that God led you to minister to today and what was their response?

_____

_____

_____

_____

_____

Who was it that ministered to you today and how did God use them in your life?

_____

_____

_____

_____

_____

_____

_____

What is the greatest spiritual lesson you learned today?

_____

_____

_____

_____

_____

_____

Share the biggest "take-away" from this day that will remind you of God's grace and faithfulness:

_____

_____

_____

_____

_____

_____

_____

_____

_____

_____

_____

Daily Schedule
Day 7 Date___/___/_____

6 am	
7 am	
8 am	
9 am	
10 am	
11 am	
12 pm	
1 pm	
2 pm	
3 pm	
4 pm	
5 pm	
6 pm	
7 pm	
8 pm	
9 pm	

Journaling Day 7   Date _____

How did God speak to you through Scripture today?

_____
_____
_____
_____
_____
_____

Where did God lead you today geographically?

_____
_____
_____
_____
_____

What has challenged your faith the most today and how can God use it in your life and ministry?

_____
_____
_____
_____
_____
_____

Who was it that God led you to minister to today and what was their response?

_____
_____
_____
_____
_____
_____

Who was it that ministered to you today and how did God use
them in your life?

_____

_____

_____

_____

_____

_____

_____

What is the greatest spiritual lesson you learned today?

_____

_____

_____

_____

_____

_____

_____

Share the biggest "take-away" from this day that will remind
you of God's grace and faithfulness:

_____

_____

_____

_____

_____

_____

_____

_____

_____

_____

_____

_____

Daily Schedule
Day 8 Date___/___/_____

6 am	
7 am	
8 am	
9 am	
10 am	
11 am	
12 pm	
1 pm	
2 pm	
3 pm	
4 pm	
5 pm	
6 pm	
7 pm	
8 pm	
9 pm	

Journaling Day 8   Date _____

How did God speak to you through Scripture today?

_____
_____
_____
_____
_____
_____

Where did God lead you today geographically?

_____
_____
_____
_____
_____

What has challenged your faith the most today and how can God use it in your life and ministry?

_____
_____
_____
_____
_____
_____

Who was it that God led you to minister to today and what was their response?

_____
_____
_____
_____
_____
_____

Who was it that ministered to you today and how did God use them in your life?

_____

_____

_____

_____

_____

_____

_____

What is the greatest spiritual lesson you learned today?

_____

_____

_____

_____

_____

_____

Share the biggest "take-away" from this day that will remind you of God's grace and faithfulness:

_____

_____

_____

_____

_____

_____

_____

_____

_____

_____

_____

_____

_____

Daily Schedule
Day 9 Date___/___/_____

6 am	
7 am	
8 am	
9 am	
10 am	
11 am	
12 pm	
1 pm	
2 pm	
3 pm	
4 pm	
5 pm	
6 pm	
7 pm	
8 pm	
9 pm	

Journaling Day 9   Date _____

How did God speak to you through Scripture today?

_____
_____
_____
_____
_____
_____

Where did God lead you today geographically?

_____
_____
_____
_____
_____

What has challenged your faith the most today and how can God use it in your life and ministry?

_____
_____
_____
_____
_____

Who was it that God led you to minister to today and what was their response?

_____
_____
_____
_____
_____

Who was it that ministered to you today and how did God use them in your life?

_____
_____
_____
_____
_____
_____
_____

What is the greatest spiritual lesson you learned today?

_____
_____
_____
_____
_____
_____

Share the biggest "take-away" from this day that will remind you of God's grace and faithfulness:

_____
_____
_____
_____
_____
_____
_____
_____
_____
_____
_____
_____

Daily Schedule
Day 10 Date___/___/_____

6 am	
7 am	
8 am	
9 am	
10 am	
11 am	
12 pm	
1 pm	
2 pm	
3 pm	
4 pm	
5 pm	
6 pm	
7 pm	
8 pm	
9 pm	

Journaling Day 10   Date _____

How did God speak to you through Scripture today?

_____

_____

_____

_____

_____

_____

Where did God lead you today geographically?

_____

_____

_____

_____

_____

What has challenged your faith the most today and how can God use it in your life and ministry?

_____

_____

_____

_____

_____

Who was it that God led you to minister to today and what was their response?

_____

_____

_____

_____

_____

Who was it that ministered to you today and how did God use them in your life?

_____

_____

_____

_____

_____

_____

_____

What is the greatest spiritual lesson you learned today?

_____

_____

_____

_____

_____

_____

_____

Share the biggest "take-away" from this day that will remind you of God's grace and faithfulness:

_____

_____

_____

_____

_____

_____

_____

_____

_____

_____

_____

_____

Daily Schedule
Day 11 Date___/___/_____

6 am	
7 am	
8 am	
9 am	
10 am	
11 am	
12 pm	
1 pm	
2 pm	
3 pm	
4 pm	
5 pm	
6 pm	
7 pm	
8 pm	
9 pm	

Journaling Day 11   Date _____

How did God speak to you through Scripture today?

_____
_____
_____
_____
_____
_____

Where did God lead you today geographically?

_____
_____
_____
_____
_____
_____

What has challenged your faith the most today and how can God use it in your life and ministry?

_____
_____
_____
_____
_____
_____

Who was it that God led you to minister to today and what was their response?

_____
_____
_____
_____
_____
_____

Who was it that ministered to you today and how did God use them in your life?

_____

_____

_____

_____

_____

_____

_____

What is the greatest spiritual lesson you learned today?

_____

_____

_____

_____

_____

_____

_____

Share the biggest "take-away" from this day that will remind you of God's grace and faithfulness:

_____

_____

_____

_____

_____

_____

_____

_____

_____

_____

_____

_____

Daily Schedule

Day 12 Date___/___/_____

6 am	
7 am	
8 am	
9 am	
10 am	
11 am	
12 pm	
1 pm	
2 pm	
3 pm	
4 pm	
5 pm	
6 pm	
7 pm	
8 pm	
9 pm	

Journaling Day 12   Date _____

How did God speak to you through Scripture today?

_____

_____

_____

_____

_____

_____

Where did God lead you today geographically?

_____

_____

_____

_____

_____

What has challenged your faith the most today and how can God use it in your life and ministry?

_____

_____

_____

_____

_____

_____

Who was it that God led you to minister to today and what was their response?

_____

_____

_____

_____

_____

Who was it that ministered to you today and how did God use
them in your life?

_____

_____

_____

_____

_____

_____

_____

What is the greatest spiritual lesson you learned today?

_____

_____

_____

_____

_____

_____

Share the biggest "take-away" from this day that will remind
you of God's grace and faithfulness:

_____

_____

_____

_____

_____

_____

_____

_____

_____

_____

_____

Daily Schedule
Day 13 Date___/___/_____

6 am	
7 am	
8 am	
9 am	
10 am	
11 am	
12 pm	
1 pm	
2 pm	
3 pm	
4 pm	
5 pm	
6 pm	
7 pm	
8 pm	
9 pm	

Journaling Day 13   Date _____

How did God speak to you through Scripture today?

_____

_____

_____

_____

_____

_____

Where did God lead you today geographically?

_____

_____

_____

_____

_____

What has challenged your faith the most today and how can God use it in your life and ministry?

_____

_____

_____

_____

_____

_____

Who was it that God led you to minister to today and what was their response?

_____

_____

_____

_____

_____

_____

Who was it that ministered to you today and how did God use them in your life?

_____

_____

_____

_____

_____

_____

_____

What is the greatest spiritual lesson you learned today?

_____

_____

_____

_____

_____

_____

_____

Share the biggest "take-away" from this day that will remind you of God's grace and faithfulness:

_____

_____

_____

_____

_____

_____

_____

_____

_____

_____

_____

Daily Schedule
Day 14 Date___/___/_____

6 am	
7 am	
8 am	
9 am	
10 am	
11 am	
12 pm	
1 pm	
2 pm	
3 pm	
4 pm	
5 pm	
6 pm	
7 pm	
8 pm	
9 pm	

Journaling Day 14   Date _____

How did God speak to you through Scripture today?

_____
_____
_____
_____
_____
_____

Where did God lead you today geographically?

_____
_____
_____
_____
_____

What has challenged your faith the most today and how can God use it in your life and ministry?

_____
_____
_____
_____
_____
_____

Who was it that God led you to minister to today and what was their response?

_____
_____
_____
_____
_____
_____

Who was it that ministered to you today and how did God use them in your life?

_____

_____

_____

_____

_____

_____

_____

What is the greatest spiritual lesson you learned today?

_____

_____

_____

_____

_____

_____

Share the biggest "take-away" from this day that will remind you of God's grace and faithfulness:

_____

_____

_____

_____

_____

_____

_____

_____

_____

_____

_____

_____

Your Mission Trip Team

Remember Your Partners in the Gospel:
The following pages are for your Team Members to share their impressions of your mission adventure. Those from the country you have come to serve are a part of your mission team too.

Ask them to write their personal information so that you can contact them in the future. It is so easy to spend all this time together and then forget to ask for their information.

Write and Draw Your Memories of People and Events:
Included on each page is quote concerning world missions by those who impacted the cause of Christ over the years, and in some cases, centuries.

You can also doodle or draw what you want to remember. Of course you want to get the contact information of your team members. But perhaps you want them to write in your journal too. Perhaps they want to share their testimony of how God worked in their lives through this trip.

You have developed new relationships through these days or weeks of working together. Your world view has been impacted too. Many who have been a part of a missions team report that they see missions in a new way.

Experience Missions in a Whole New Way :
Most important of all is that through this experience, your spiritual relationship to Christ has deepened, that you have been changed for the better!

You will pray at a deeper level too. Your prayer life will take on a whole new dimension because of your involvement in the Great Commission.

You will read the Bible through a new lens, especially the Book of Acts. You will appreciate the journaling efforts of Luke to capture what God was doing through those first Mission Trip Teams!

My Mission Trip Team

"He is no fool who gives up what he cannot keep to gain
that which he cannot lose" — Jim Elliot

Contact Information and Impressions of Your Time Together
Doodle or Draw a Picture of What you Want to Remember

My Mission Trip Team

"If a commission by an earthly king is considered a honor, how can a commission by a Heavenly King be considered a sacrifice?"
— David Livingstone

Contact Information and Impressions of Your Time Together
Doodle or Draw a Picture of What you Want to Remember

My Mission Trip Team

"Some wish to live within the sound of a chapel bell. I wish to run a rescue mission within a yard of hell." — C.T. Studd

Contact Information and Impressions of Your Time Together
Doodle or Draw a Picture of What you Want to Remember

My Mission Trip Team

"Let my heart be broken with the things that break God's heart"
— Bob Pierce, World Vision founder

Contact Information and Impressions of Your Time Together
Doodle or Draw a Picture of What you Want to Remember

My Mission Trip Team

"The reason some folks don't believe in missions is that the brand of religion they have isn't worth propagating." — unknown

Contact Information and Impressions of Your Time Together
Doodle or Draw a Picture of What you Want to Remember

My Mission Trip Team

"The gospel is only good news if it gets there in time"
— Carl F. H. Henry

Contact Information and Impressions of Your Time Together
Doodle or Draw a Picture of What you Want to Remember

My Mission Trip Team

"The mark of a great church is not its seating capacity,
but its sending capacity." — Mike Stachura

Contact Information and Impressions of Your Time Together
Doodle or Draw a Picture of What you Want to Remember

My Mission Trip Team

"Never pity missionaries, envy them. They are where the real action is — where life and death, sin and grace, heaven and hell converge."
— Robert C. Shannon

Contact Information and Impressions of Your Time Together
Doodle or Draw a Picture of What you Want to Remember

My Mission Trip Team

"If you take missions out of the Bible, you won't have anything left but the covers" — Nina Gunter

Contact Information and Impressions of Your Time Together
Doodle or Draw a Picture of What you Want to Remember

My Mission Trip Team

Information "The average pastor views his church as a local church with a missions program, while he ought to realize that if he is in fact pastoring a church, it is to be a global church with a missions purpose." — Unknown

Contact Information and Impressions of Your Time Together
Doodle or Draw a Picture of What you Want to Remember

My Mission Trip Team

"Without a vision the people perish and without the people, the vision perishes." – Anonymous

Contact Information and Impressions of Your Time Together
Doodle or Draw a Picture of What you Want to Remember

My Mission Trip Team

"Only as the church fulfills her missionary obligation does she justify her existence." – Anonymous

Contact Information and Impressions of Your Time Together
Doodle or Draw a Picture of What you Want to Remember

My Mission Trip Team

"God does not put an age limit on fulfilling the Great Commission."

- - Anonymous

Contact Information and Impressions of Your Time Together
Doodle or Draw a Picture of What you Want to Remember

My Mission Trip Team

"Here is a test to find whether your mission on earth is finished: If you are alive, it isn't." - Richard Bach

Contact Information and Impressions of Your Time Together
Doodle or Draw a Picture of What you Want to Remember

My Mission Trip Team

"Expect great things from God, attempt great things for God."
-- William Carey

Contact Information and Impressions of Your Time Together
Doodle or Draw a Picture of What you Want to Remember

My Mission Trip Team

"To know the will of God, we need an open Bible and an open map."
-- William Carey

Contact Information and Impressions of Your Time Together
Doodle or Draw a Picture of What you Want to Remember

My Mission Trip Team

"Whom shall I send, and who will go for us?" – God
"Here am I. Send me." – Isaiah

Contact Information and Impressions of Your Time Together
Doodle or Draw a Picture of What you Want to Remember

My Mission Trip Team

"This gospel of the kingdom shall be preached in all the world as a witness unto all nations, and then the end shall come." --Jesus

Contact Information and Impressions of Your Time Together
Doodle or Draw a Picture of What you Want to Remember

My Mission Trip Team

"The mission of the church is missions." - Oswald J. Smith

Contact Information and Impressions of Your Time Together
Doodle or Draw a Picture of What you Want to Remember

My Mission Trip Team

"We should not ask, 'What is wrong with the world?' for that diagnosis has already been given. Rather, we should ask, 'What happened to the salt and light?'" - John Stott

Contact Information and Impressions of Your Time Together
Doodle or Draw a Picture of What you Want to Remember

Reporting Back What God Did on This Mission Trip

The Mission Trip may be over but God's Mission continues on in the lives of those whose lives were impacted for Christ through your efforts.

The Biblical Basis for Reporting Back
Notice that in the Book of Acts those on those Early Church Mission Teams reported back what they had experienced.

> Acts 14:26-27 WEB
> (26) From there they sailed to Antioch, from where they had been committed to the grace of God for the work which they had fulfilled.
> (27) When they had arrived, and had gathered the assembly together, **they reported all the things that God had done** with them, and that he had opened a door of faith to the nations.

> Acts 21:19 WEB
> (19) When he had greeted them, he **reported one by one the things which God had worked** among the Gentiles through his ministry.

The Content of the Report
Just as Luke had documented the mission trips of Acts, so you too have documented your mission trip. In your report, whether to individuals or groups of people, this journal is your resource for what you will say.

- Tell about changed lives because of God's grace being shared. You have names and locations, events and work assignments written down, so include them in your report.

- Share how God has changed you through this trip. You have seen God work in your perspective on missions and how God has used you. Report what God is doing spiritually within you because of this trip.

Events, People, and Places I Want to "Report Back"

_____

_____

_____

_____

_____

_____

_____

_____

_____

_____

_____

_____

_____

_____

_____

_____

_____

_____

_____

_____

_____

_____

Events, People, and Places I Want to "Report Back"

_____

_____

_____

_____

_____

_____

_____

_____

_____

_____

_____

_____

_____

_____

_____

_____

_____

_____

_____

_____

_____

_____

_____

_____

_____

Events, People, and Places I Want to "Report Back"

_____

_____

_____

_____

_____

_____

_____

_____

_____

_____

_____

_____

_____

_____

_____

_____

_____

_____

_____

_____

_____

Events, People, and Places I Want to "Report Back"

_____

_____

_____

_____

_____

_____

_____

_____

_____

_____

_____

_____

_____

_____

_____

_____

_____

_____

_____

_____

_____

_____

Events, People, and Places I Want to "Report Back"

_____

_____

_____

_____

_____

_____

_____

_____

_____

_____

_____

_____

_____

_____

_____

_____

_____

_____

_____

_____

_____

_____

_____

Events, People, and Places I Want to "Report Back"

_____

_____

_____

_____

_____

_____

_____

_____

_____

_____

_____

_____

_____

_____

_____

_____

_____

_____

_____

_____

_____

_____

_____

_____

Events, People, and Places I Want to "Report Back"

_____

_____

_____

_____

_____

_____

_____

_____

_____

_____

_____

_____

_____

_____

_____

_____

_____

_____

_____

_____

Events, People, and Places I Want to "Report Back"

_____

_____

_____

_____

_____

_____

_____

_____

_____

_____

_____

_____

_____

_____

_____

_____

_____

_____

_____

_____

_____

_____

_____

_____

Events, People, and Places I Want to "Report Back"

_____

_____

_____

_____

_____

_____

_____

_____

_____

_____

_____

_____

_____

_____

_____

_____

_____

_____

_____

_____

_____

_____

_____

Events, People, and Places I Want to "Report Back"

_____

_____

_____

_____

_____

_____

_____

_____

_____

_____

_____

_____

_____

_____

_____

_____

_____

_____

_____

_____

_____

_____

Events, People, and Places I Want to "Report Back"

_____

_____

_____

_____

_____

_____

_____

_____

_____

_____

_____

_____

_____

_____

_____

_____

_____

_____

_____

_____

_____

_____

_____

_____

_____

Events, People, and Places I Want to "Report Back"

_____

_____

_____

_____

_____

_____

_____

_____

_____

_____

_____

_____

_____

_____

_____

_____

_____

_____

_____

_____

_____

Events, People, and Places I Want to "Report Back"

_____

_____

_____

_____

_____

_____

_____

_____

_____

_____

_____

_____

_____

_____

_____

_____

_____

_____

_____

_____

_____

_____

Events, People, and Places I Want to "Report Back"

_____

_____

_____

_____

_____

_____

_____

_____

_____

_____

_____

_____

_____

_____

_____

_____

_____

_____

_____

_____

_____

_____

_____

Events, People, and Places I Want to "Report Back"

_____

_____

_____

_____

_____

_____

_____

_____

_____

_____

_____

_____

_____

_____

_____

_____

_____

_____

_____

_____

_____

_____

Events, People, and Places I Want to "Report Back"

_____

_____

_____

_____

_____

_____

_____

_____

_____

_____

_____

_____

_____

_____

_____

_____

_____

_____

_____

_____

_____

_____

_____

_____

Events, People, and Places I Want to "Report Back"

_____

_____

_____

_____

_____

_____

_____

_____

_____

_____

_____

_____

_____

_____

_____

_____

_____

_____

_____

_____

_____

_____

Events, People, and Places I Want to "Report Back"

_____

_____

_____

_____

_____

_____

_____

_____

_____

_____

_____

_____

_____

_____

_____

_____

_____

_____

_____

_____

Events, People, and Places I Want to "Report Back"

_____

_____

_____

_____

_____

_____

_____

_____

_____

_____

_____

_____

_____

_____

_____

_____

_____

_____

_____

_____

_____

_____

How Does this Mission Quote
Challenge You Spiritually?

"Go and make disciples of all nations, baptizing them in the name of the Father and of the Son and of the Holy Spirit, teaching them to observe all things that I commanded you. Behold, I am with you always, even to the end of the age." (Matthew 28:19-20 WEB

_____

_____

_____

_____

_____

"The Great Commission is not an option to be considered, it is a command to be obeyed" — Hudson Taylor

_____

_____

_____

_____

_____

"Expect great things from God—attempt great things for God. Expect great things from God—receive great things from God. Expect little from God—receive little from God." William Carey

_____

_____

_____

_____

_____

How Does this Mission Quote Challenge You to Obey the Great Commission?

"Vision attracts resources.
Sacrifice inspires others to participate.
Perseverance gives God time to work in our behalf."
Larry J. Webb

"We should not ask, 'What is wrong with the world?' for that diagnosis has already been given. Rather, we should ask, 'What happened to the salt and light?'" - John Stott

---

"I have found that there are three stages in every great work of God. First, it is impossible, then it is difficult, then it is done."
- Hudson Taylor

How Does this Mission Quote Challenge You to Obey the Great Commission?

"To know the will of God, we need an open Bible and an open map."
- William Carey;

_____

_____

_____

_____

_____

"The average pastor views his church as a local church with a missions program, while he ought to realize that if he is in fact pastoring a church, it is to be a global church with a missions purpose." — Unknown

_____

_____

_____

_____

_____

"God does not put an age limit on fulfilling the Great Commission." - Anonymous

_____

_____

_____

_____

_____

Made in the USA
Monee, IL
29 June 2024